HARRIET BEECHER STOWE'S

Story to End Slavery

Women's Biographies Grade 5
Children's Biographies

DISSECTED LIVES
auto biographies

First Edition, 2020

Published in the United States by Speedy Publishing LLC, 40 E Main Street, Newark, Delaware 19711 USA.

© 2020 Dissected Lives Books, an imprint of Speedy Publishing LLC

Dissected Lives Books are available at special discounts when purchased in bulk for industrial and sales-promotional use. For details contact our Special Sales Team at Speedy Publishing LLC, 40 E Main Street, Newark, Delaware 19711 USA. Telephone (888) 248-4521 Fax: (210) 519-4043. www.speedybookstore.com

10 9 8 7 6 * 5 4 3 2 1

Print Edition: 9781541960596
Digital Edition: 9781541963597

See the world in pictures. Build your knowledge in style.
www.speedypublishing.com

Table of Contents

HARRIET BEECHER STOWE'S

Story to End Slavery

Women's Biographies Grade 5
Children's Biographies

Many people have heard it said that "from a tiny seed a big tree can grow." This expression can be used to encourage a person to stand up and do great things even when it seems next to impossible to make a change. One such person who took a big step to make a difference was an American author from the 1800s. This woman was Harriet Beecher Stowe and she wrote a book which had an enormous impact on societal views on slavery. The book is entitled Uncle Tom's Cabin.

In the next pages, you will read about the author, what influenced her to write her book, and how it was received by people and how it played a role in influencing the American Civil War.

Harriet Beecher Stowe

Who was Harriet Beecher Stowe?

Young Harriet Beecher

Harriet Beecher Stowe was born on June 14, 1811 and was christened Harriet Elizabeth Beecher. Her father was Lyman Beecher and he was a well-known Presbyterian preacher. Her mother's name was Roxanna Foote Beecher.

HARRIET BEECHER STOWE'S

Story to End Slavery

Women's Biographies Grade 5
Children's Biographies

Connecticut, Litchfield
Hills, USA

The family lived in Litchfield, Connecticut and that is where Harriet Beecher Stowe was born. Her parents were very religious people whose morals and beliefs in social reforms strongly influenced the young Harriet.

Harriet was alive during the time of the temperance movement, a movement that was against the production, selling and consumption of alcohol, and her father was an active supporter of the movement.

Temperance poster promoting the prohibition of alcohol

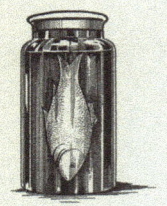

ALCOHOL

A BLESSING

A CURSE

WHISKY

GOOD FOR THE ENGINE, BUT NOT FOR THE ENGINEER

GOOD FOR COMMERCIAL PURPOSES, BUT NOT AS A BEVERAGE

Published by The Dominion Scientific Temperance Committee   Temperance Lesson No. 4

Harriet had a sister, Catherine, who was the founder of a school in Hartford, Connecticut. Harriet moved there during her childhood.

Catherine Beecher

While there, Catherine's education reforms had a positive impact on Harriet. Harriet was able to study and she excelled at writing. She later became a teacher at the school.

Harriet excelled in writing and became a teacher

When she was barely out of her teen years, Harriet moved to Ohio with her family. Being not too far from the Ohio River, Harriet went to the side of the river to enjoy the scenery.

Harriet Beecher Stowe House in Cincinnati, OH

What she saw shocked and disturbed her. Instead of just observing boats leisurely pass by, Harriet noticed that the boats were full of slaves. To make matters worse, the slaves were in chains.

Slaves chained

Harriet soon learned that there were slaves in the state of Kentucky.

Kentucky state was one of the first producers of Hemp fiber used for paper and clothes. Production was a hard and tedious process, with only the slaves working on fields

The people on board the boats were being shipped to different places to be sold into slavery. Not only were the traveling conditions bad, but life as a slave under an owner was awful as well.

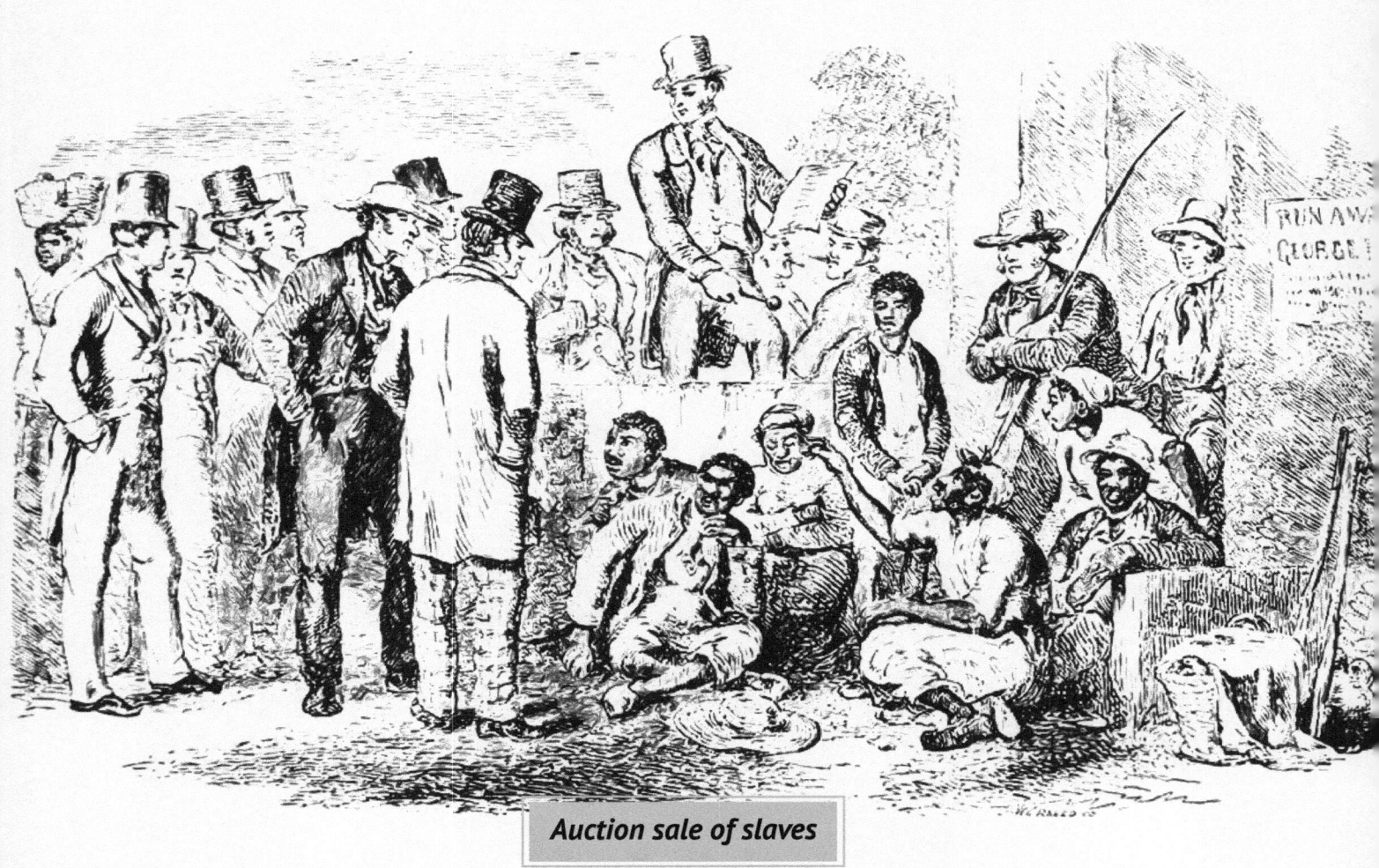

Auction sale of slaves

Harriet became deeply concerned for the people who were forced into slavery. It made an impact on her because it was the first time that she had been so close to it.

Harriet became distressed upon seeing people forced into slavery

Until moving to Ohio, Harriet had only heard about slavery. She had not witnessed slavery because she lived in a free state. The sudden exposure to slavery opened her eyes to the horrors of it. Harriet's life would not be the same again.

Slave trade

After having been in Ohio for roughly four years, Harriet got married. Her husband's name was Calvin Stowe and he held the positions of both minister and professor. They lived in Cincinnati.

Calvin Ellis Stowe

HARRIET BEECHER STOWE'S

Story to End Slavery

Women's Biographies Grade 5
Children's Biographies

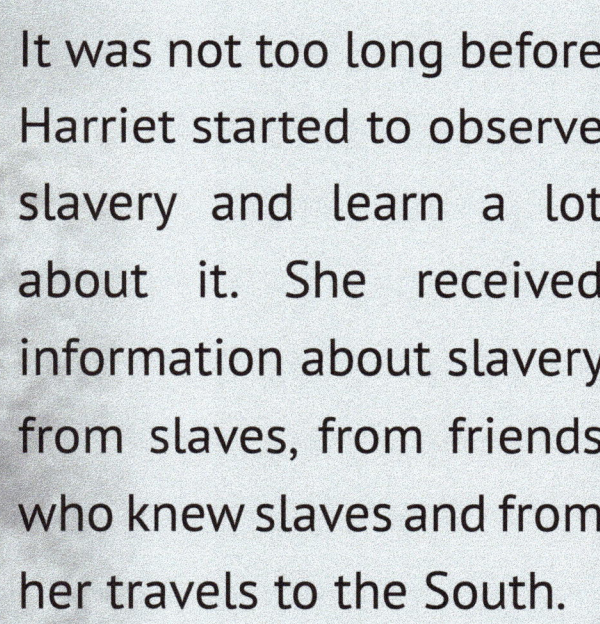

It was not too long before Harriet started to observe slavery and learn a lot about it. She received information about slavery from slaves, from friends who knew slaves and from her travels to the South.

Family of slaves in Georgia, 1850

In 1850, Harriet and Calvin moved to Brunswick, Maine where Calvin became a college professor.

Harriet Beecher Stowe House
Brunswick, Maine

Underground
road

HARRIET BEECHER STOWE'S

Story to End Slavery

Women's Biographies Grade 5
Children's Biographies

Harriet started to meet slaves who had run away from their masters. The fugitive slaves wanted to have better lives. One day, Harriet discovered that one of the servants who she and her husband had employed was in fact a runaway slave. Harriet and Calvin decided that they would help their servant find freedom.

Harriet and Calvin helped their servant find freedom

HISTORIC UNDERGROUND RAILROAD

THE UNDERGROUND RAILROAD

The Underground Railroad was neither underground nor a railroad, but a system of loosely connected safe havens where those escaping the brutal conditions of slavery were sheltered, fed, clothed, nursed, concealed, disguised, and instructed during their journey to freedom. Although this movement was one of America's greatest social, moral, and humanitarian endeavors, the details about it were often cloaked in secrecy to protect those involved from the retribution of civil law and slave-catchers.

Ohio's history has been permanently shaped by the thousands of runaway slaves passing through or finding permanent residence in this state.

CO-SPONSORSHIP OF ODOT AND FRIENDS OF FREEDOM SOCIETY

HISTORIC UNDERGROUND RAILROAD

DELAWARE COUNTY: ANTI-SLAVERY STRONGHOLD

A unique combination of strong-principled religious communities, free black settlements, and tightly knit extended families fostered a wide-spread attitude of willful defiance that made Delaware one of Ohio's strongest anti-slavery counties in the early nineteenth century.

Among the Delaware County congregations participating in the Underground Railroad were Berlin United Presbyterian, Wesleyan Methodist, Alum Creek, Friends and Otterbein's United Brethren.

Manumitted slaves who settled the hamlet of Africa, at the intersection of present day Polaris parkway and Africa Road in southeastern Delaware County, and those who came to the area with early white settlers. John McClure and Benjamin Bartholomew, had a fierce hatred of bondage, they helped escaping slaves whenever possible. Bartholomew and his son, Major Bartholomew, operated a station near the Olentangy River in southern Liberty Township.

Sometimes more than one member of a family participated in the Underground Railroad. Northern Delaware County resident, William Cratty, epitomized local attitudes by publicly denouncing the unjust Fugitive Slave Law of 1850. He vowed to continue to "run slaves" and he did not care who knew it "in congress or out!" Aided by his brother, John and sister, Peggy, Cratty claimed to have assisted three-thousand fugitives to Canada. The bounty on Cratty's head was $3,000, dead or alive.

Other local Delaware stations were Halfway House, George Gooding's tavern on State Route 23, and Seven Oaks on William Street.

CO-SPONSORSHIP OF ODOT AND FRIENDS OF FREEDOM SOCIETY

They helped their servant make it to the Underground Railroad. The Underground Railroad was the term given to the help that the abolitionists, people who wanted to outlaw slavery, gave to slaves who were trying to flee their masters.

Underground Railroad Historical mark, Delaware County

Abolitionist helping fugitive slaves

The abolitionists would secretly work with fugitive slaves and other abolitionists to secure a secret route for fugitive slaves to leave their masters in the South and travel to states in the North or to Canada.

Armed fugitive slave family defending themselves against slave catchers

One of the challenges was to evade the slave hunters who tried to find the fugitive slaves and return them to the dreadful conditions under slave owners.

HARRIET BEECHER STOWE'S

Story to End Slavery

Women's Biographies Grade 5
Children's Biographies

Nonetheless, thousands of fugitive slaves successfully fled their masters with the assistance of the Underground Railroad.

The Underground Railroad

Harriet Beecher Stowe's Involvement in the Anti-Slavery Movement

Harriet was increasingly disturbed by the concept of slavery. She was completely against it. The more exposure she had to fugitive slaves, the more heartbreaking stories she heard of the disgusting treatment that many slaves received.

Group of slaves escaping for the North in the night

Harriet and Calvin became parents to seven children. One of their children, a son, died in childhood. It was upon grieving the loss of her son that she began to empathize with the loss that slaves endured regularly.

Harriet and Calvin

In addition to other acts of cruelty, slaves often lost contact with their loved ones when slave owners sold members of the same families to other slave owners. Harriet could no longer take the strong feelings of disdain for the immoral act of slavery. It was time for her to do something.

Slave owners sold members of the same families to other slave owners

Harriet started to write about the horrors of slavery. In addition to focusing on different slave families, her famous book, Uncle Tom's Cabin, talks about the character, Tom, and his life.

Harriet Beecher Stowe, wrote Uncle Tom's Cabin while living in Brunswick, Maine

It described what it was like for Tom to be a slave. He was forced to be a slave to three different slave owners. The third slave owner was so bad to Tom that he died a cruel death at the slave owner's hand.

The Death of Uncle Tom

The story, nonetheless, has a good ending because it also talks about how an entire family flees slavery and makes it across the border to Canada.

Entire family flees slavery

At first the story was published in segments, with one chapter being printed at a time in a newspaper. Later, the chapters were compiled into a book. The compiled chapters, Uncle Tom's Cabin, was published in 1852. There were two main reactions to the book when it was first published, those who supported it and those who did not.

Uncle Tom's Cabin, published in 1852

Many people who lived in the North became drawn to the story and its anti-slavery theme. The ending of the book encouraged people to assist fugitive slaves in their effort to flee their owners.

Uncle Tom's Cabin Lithograph showing Eliza and her baby running to freedom across the frozen Ohio river

This was not always easy to do because of the Fugitive Slave Act. This act allowed slaves to be captured, even in the North, and to be returned to their slave owners in the South.

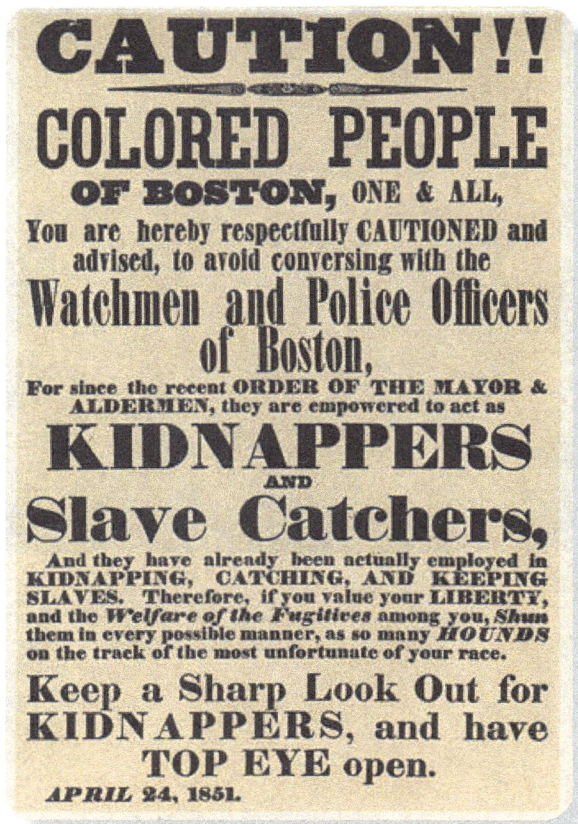

A poster dated April 24, 1851 warning colored people in Boston to beware of authorities who acted as slave catchers

Those who did not oppose slavery, criticized the book. They claimed that the book was not a true indication of how slaves were treated.

An image of idealized portrayal of American slavery. A group of happy slaves dance in the background

HARRIET BEECHER STOWE'S
Story to End Slavery

Women's Biographies Grade 5
Children's Biographies

HARRIET BEECHER STOWE'S

Story to End Slavery

Women's Biographies Grade 5
Children's Biographies

Some slave owners reportedly claimed that slavery was a help to slaves as it provided them with employment and living quarters. They tried to argue that slaves were being helped by this living arrangement. The book was even banned in some places in the South.

Slave owners claimed that they helped slaves with employment and living quarters.

HARRIET BEECHER STOWE'S

Story to End Slavery

Women's Biographies Grade 5
Children's Biographies

However, the story was believed by many and its publication is said to have been an influence in the American Civil War. It helped to open people's eyes to the many horrors that slaves had to endure.

The book, Uncle Tom's Cabin, is believed to have an influence in the American Civil War

Before long, the book became a bestseller and it has been translated into many different languages. It has also found its way into the curriculum of many schools.

Different versions of the book Uncle Tom's Cabin

The Impact of Uncle Tom's Cabin on the American Civil War

Because *Uncle Tom's Cabin* gained such popularity, it helped to educate people about the cruel and immoral act of slavery. It also started to divide the opinions of those in the North with those in the South.

HARRIET BEECHER STOWE'S

Story to End Slavery

Women's Biographies Grade 5
Children's Biographies

A modern screen version of the everalsting play Uncle Tom's cabin

The topic of slavery was one of the reasons for the civil war. Many people in the northern states were against slavery and they wanted it to be formally abolished nationwide. This part of the country was where the abolitionists had a stronghold.

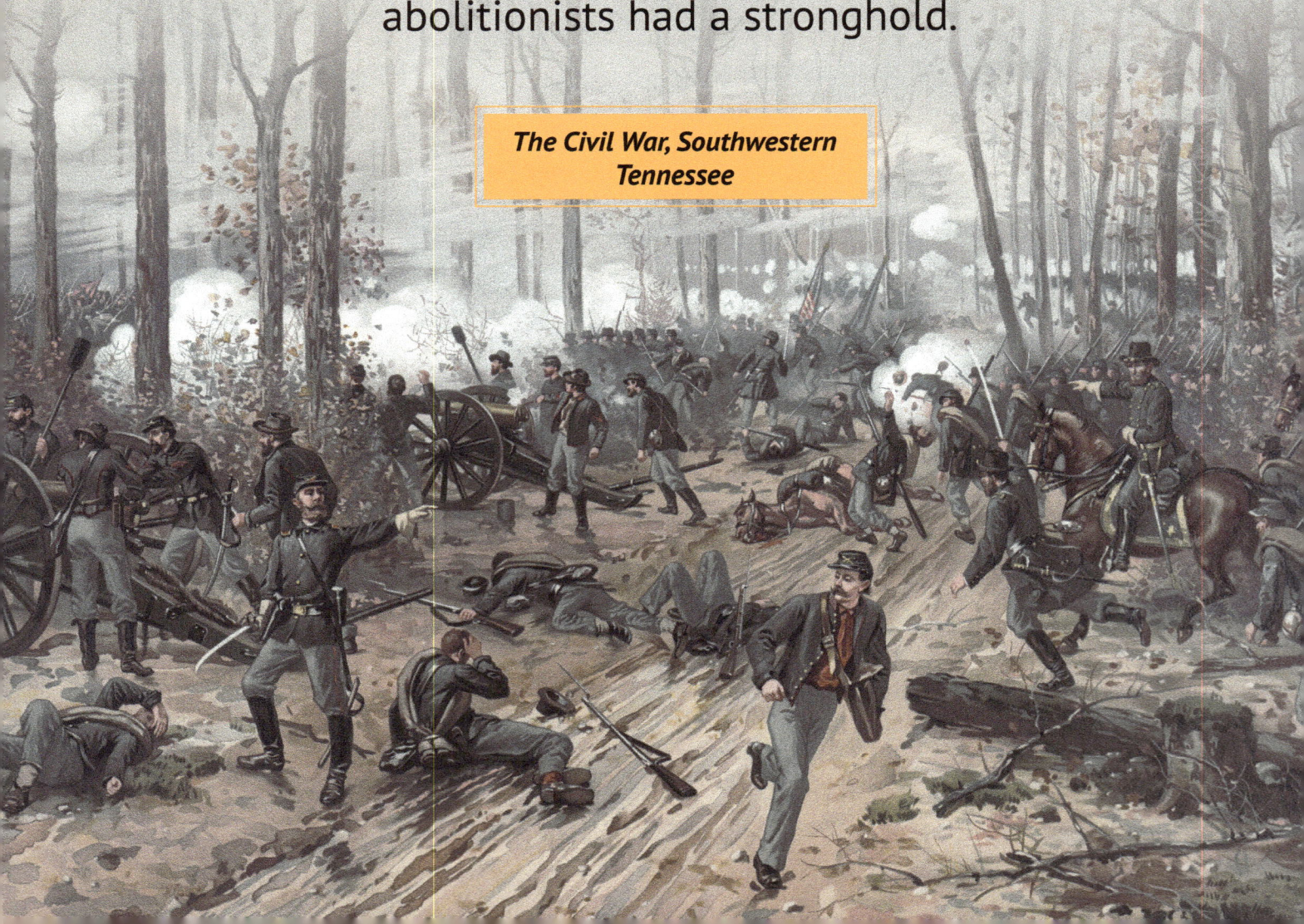

The Civil War, Southwestern Tennessee

In 1833, William Lloyd Garrison founded the American Anti-Slavery Society. Although the abolitionists did not always agree on the way in which slavery should be stopped, they all shared a strong disdain for it.

William Lloyd Garrison, founder of American Anti-Slavery Society

They knew that something had to be done to stop this evil. All of the states north of Maryland had ended slavery by 1804.

A map showing the parts of the US that are Free States

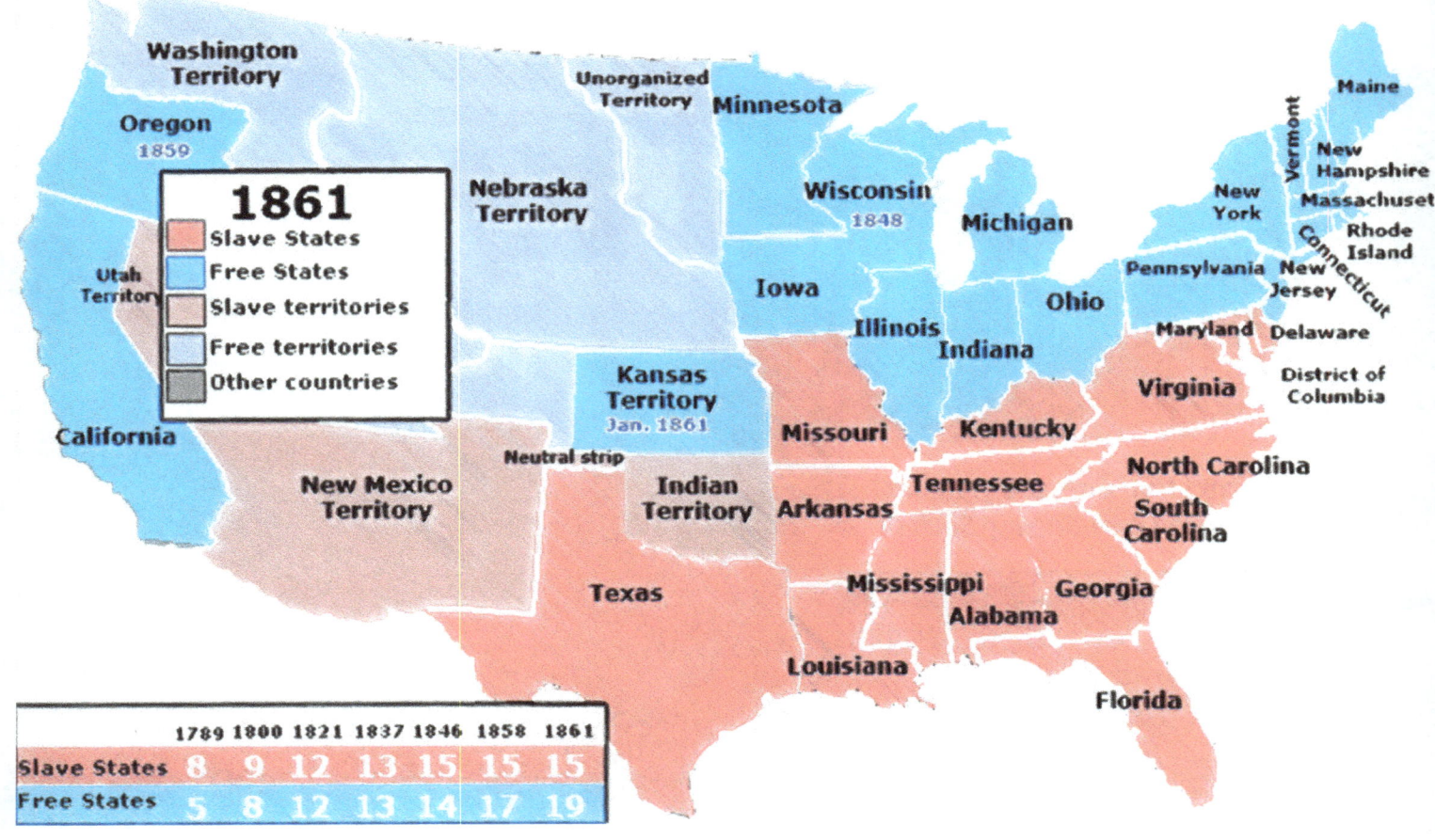

	1789	1800	1821	1837	1846	1858	1861
Slave States	8	9	12	13	15	15	15
Free States	5	8	12	13	14	17	19

The southern states, where many plantations were located, were not in favor of ending slavery. Slavery enabled the economies in the South to flourish.

Slaves working on a plantation in a southern state of the United States of America

Maintaining a good economy through slavery and having the political control to do so were two reasons for which the South was prepared to take up arms. Developing and maintaining plantations provided the need for more and more slaves.

Slaves labour loading sacks of cotton on cart, Southern States of USA

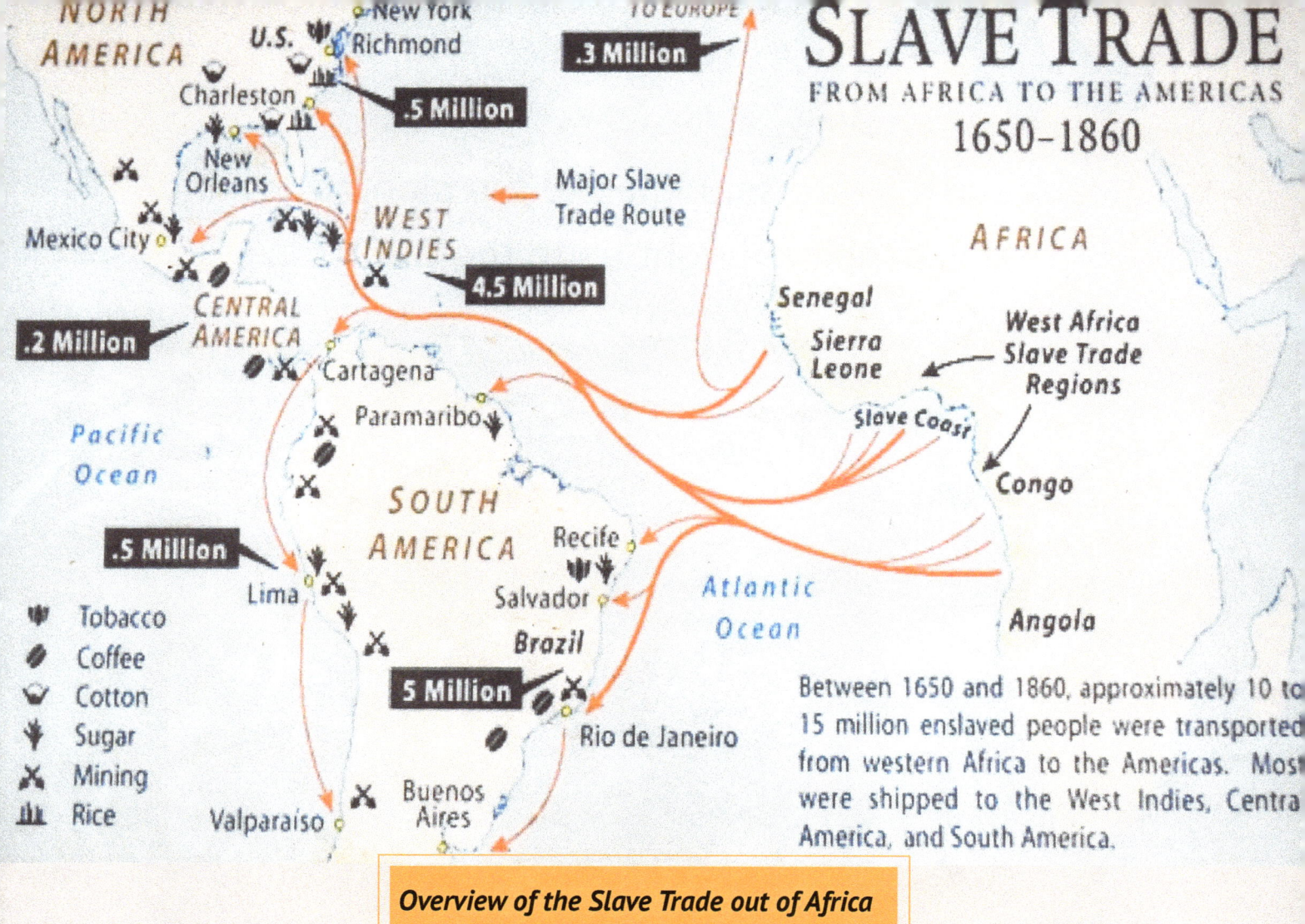

NORTH AMERICA

U.S. — New York / Richmond

.3 Million — TO EUROPE

.5 Million

Charleston

New Orleans

Mexico City

Major Slave Trade Route

WEST INDIES

4.5 Million

CENTRAL AMERICA

.2 Million

Cartagena

Paramaribo

Pacific Ocean

SOUTH AMERICA

Recife

Salvador

Brazil

5 Million

Rio de Janeiro

.5 Million

Lima

Atlantic Ocean

Valparaíso

Buenos Aires

Tobacco
Coffee
Cotton
Sugar
Mining
Rice

SLAVE TRADE
FROM AFRICA TO THE AMERICAS
1650–1860

AFRICA

Senegal

Sierra Leone

West Africa Slave Trade Regions

Slave Coast

Congo

Angola

Between 1650 and 1860, approximately 10 to 15 million enslaved people were transported from western Africa to the Americas. Most were shipped to the West Indies, Central America, and South America.

Overview of the Slave Trade out of Africa

Despite the United States having adopted the Slave Trade Act on March 2, 1807 in which it became illegal to participate in the Atlantic slave trade, the trading of slaves within the U.S. itself still occurred in certain states.

Many slaves were smuggled to the plantations and this happened right up to the Civil War.

Slaves unloading sacks of cotton for processing, Southern States of USA

Abraham Lincoln Becomes the President of the United States

Abraham Lincoln was elected by the American people as their president in November,1860. He was against slavery and his anti-slavery belief was made known in his political platform when he ran for office.

Abraham Lincoln

"I, Abraham Lincoln . . . declare that all persons held as slaves within said designated States and parts of States are, and henceforward shall be, free."
—The Emancipation Proclamation, January 1, 1863

His anti-slavery view made many southerners nervous. They feared that he would outlaw slavery.

Emancipation poster on President Lincoln in Gettysburg museum

The slave owners relied heavily on the work of the slaves to cultivate their fields, especially the cotton fields. Within a period of three months, many of the states in the south withdrew from the United States and created the Confederacy. They were prepared to go to war with the North.

The Southern Confederacy - Senate Chamber in the Capitol at Montgomery, Alabama

Civil War, Rhode Island

In 1861, the American Civil War started. It lasted until 1865, when the Confederacy had to admit defeat.

However, while the civil war was still raging on, Abraham Lincoln declared an executive order, the Emancipation Proclamation. In this presidential proclamation, on September 22, 1862, it was ordered that all slaves were to be freed.

First reading of Emancipation Proclamation before the cabinet, July 22, 1862. L to R: Edwin Stanton, Salmon Chase, Lincoln, Gideon Wells, Caleb Smith, William Seward, Montgomery Blair, Edward Bates

The Proclamation came into effect on New Year's Day, 1863.

Shortly after the Emancipation Proclamation went into effect on January 1, 1863 many freed slaves escaped to the Union Army lines at Newbern.

64

AMENDMENT 13

(Ratified December 6, 1865)

Section 1. Neither slavery nor involuntary servitude, except as a punishment for crime whereof the party shall have been duly convicted, shall exist within the United States, or any place subject to their jurisdiction.

Section 2. Congress shall have power to enforce this arti-appropriate legislation.

AMENDMENT 14

Further to that, on December 6, 1865, the 13th Amendment to the Constitution of the United States of America was ratified. Slavery was officially ended.

Uncle Tom's Cabin had become so popular that Harriet Beecher Stowe had the opportunity to meet President Abraham Lincoln while the Civil War was being fought. During their encounter, President Lincoln said that a lot of people were influenced by the content of her anti-slavery book.

A statue of Abraham Lincoln meeting Harriet Beecher Stowe, Hartford Connecticut.

Harriet Beecher Stowe's Legacy

Harriet Beecher Stowe demonstrated that one person can accomplish great things and influence societal change. *Uncle Tom's Cabin* showed that slavery was not only wrong for the people who were slaves, but it was wrong for those who tolerated it.

Harriet Beecher Stowe

OHIO

HISTORICAL
MARKER

HARRIET BEECHER STOWE

Harriet Beecher Stowe was born in Litchfield, Connecticut in 1811 and moved to Cincinnati in 1832 when her father, prominent Congregational minister Lyman Beecher became the pastor of the city's Second Presbyterian Church and president of Lane Theological Seminary. Married to Calvin E. Stowe in 1836, she bore six of the couple's seven children while living here. Life in the city provided Stowe with the firsthand accounts about the evils of slavery. Already a published writer, she drew upon these experiences and the death of her infant son Charley in 1849 to write *Uncle Tom's Cabin*. Published in book form in 1852, *Uncle Tom's Cabin* almost single-handedly popularized the cause of anti-slavery, made Stowe famous, and remains an icon of the American anti-slavery movement. A prolific writer, she wrote a book a year for nearly thirty years of her life. After moving from Cincinnati in 1850, the Stowes lived in Brunswick, Maine, Andover, Massachusetts, and Hartford, Connecticut, where she died in 1896.

OHIO BICENTENNIAL COMMISSION
THE CINCINNATI FOUNDATION
2001   THE OHIO HISTORICAL SOCIETY   29-31

Harriet Beecher Stowe had a writing career that spanned over half a century. In addition to her famous novel, *Uncle Tom's Cabin*, she is credited with having written over thirty books in total. She also had many articles published during her writing career.

Harriet Beecher Stowe Historical Marker.Cincinnati, Hamilton County, Ohio

Harriet Beecher Stowe died on July 1, 1896 in Hartford, Connecticut. The words she penned many years ago are still being read today.

Visit

www.speedypublishing.com

to download Free Baby Professor eBooks and view our catalog of new and exciting Children's Books